No Lex 1/13

Natural Wonders
of America

Natural Wonders of America

David M. Brownstone

Irene M. Franck

ALADDIN BOOKS
Macmillan Publishing Company · New York

For Becky, Daniel, and Jane

Aladdin Books
Macmillan Publishing Company
866 Third Avenue, New York, NY 10022
Collier Macmillan Canada, Inc.

First Aladdin Books edition 1989

Printed in the United States of America

A hardcover edition of *Natural Wonders of America* is available from Atheneum, Macmillan Publishing Company.

10 9 8 7 6 5 4 3 2 1

Library of Congress Cataloging-in-Publication Data
Brownstone, David M.
Natural wonders of America.
Includes index.
Summary: Describes the unique physical features, wildlife, plants, and discovery of such natural wonders as the Grand Canyon, Niagara Falls, Carlsbad Caverns, Mount McKinley, Death Valley, Cape Breton, Kilauea Volcano, and the Everglades.
1. Natural history—United States—Juvenile literature. 2. National parks and reserves—United States—Juvenile literature. 3. Natural monuments—United States—Juvenile literature. [1. Natural history. 2. National parks and reserves. 3. Natural monuments] I. Franck, Irene M. II. Title.
[QH104.B777 1989b]   508.73   88-32707
ISBN 0-689-71229-4

Contents

Preface

In this book, you will see and read about many of America's greatest natural wonders. Here are the Grand Canyon and Niagara Falls, Carlsbad Caverns and Mount McKinley, Death Valley and Cape Breton, Kilauea Volcano and the huge Everglades swamp—and much, much more. Here, too, you will find the stories of many of the explorers and naturalists who discovered and preserved these places for all of us—people like Zebulon Pike, who found Pikes Peak, and John Muir, who found and saved wonderful Yosemite Valley.

In *Natural Wonders of America*, words and pictures give the flavor of each place and tell why the place is so special or important. The pictures, in full color, are drawn from all over North America and beyond. Throughout, we have focused on places that people can not only *see*, but can also—perhaps later—visit. The places are grouped in alphabetical order. As a reference guide, a full index is also provided at the back of the book.

We hope that you will enjoy *Natural Wonders of America* and that reading the book will make you want to visit as many of these places as you can.

The rugged peaks of Acadia overlook the Atlantic Ocean.

Acadia National Park

At Acadia National Park, the steep, rocky shore of Maine drops right down to the waters of the North Atlantic. This is a place of mountains, sea, sky, a variety of wildlife, and the constant roar of the surf. Acadia offers the visitor a striking seashore and a wonderful wildlife preserve, too.

For centuries, this was the land of the Abnaki Indian people. French explorer Samuel de Champlain first came to this section of Maine's Atlantic coast in 1604 and was struck by the bare, treeless peaks of the mountains. So he named the main island *L'Isle des Mont Déserts*, meaning "the Island of the Bare Peaks." Later, Maine became part of the English American colonies, and the island was called, in English, Mount Desert Island.

Cadillac Mountain here is over fifteen hundred feet high. That is not very high, compared to the towering mountains of the western United States. But it is the highest place on the whole Atlantic coast. From the top of Cadillac Mountain, you can enjoy a fine view of much of the rocky coastline and see far out to sea.

Among the wildlife you can see at Acadia are eagles, ospreys, black ducks, warblers, and many other kinds of birds. Some of the birds live here all year, while others fly far south for the winter. In the sea, you can see whales, porpoises, and harbor seals. The Acadian coast is also the home of the famous Maine lobster, along with crabs, mussels, sea snails, and other kinds of shellfish.

Arches

Wind-cut sandstone rocks form the Arches.

Arches National Park is a dry and dusty desert, full of red sandstone, sagebrush, and cactus. Yet it is also a strange and very beautiful place.

This national park in Utah is full of thousands of sandstone arches, of all sizes and shapes. These arches have been cut out of thick sandstone that was part of an ocean floor millions of years ago, by the action of water on the stone. No river or stream has worn away the stone, as at Niagara Falls, Bryce Canyon, or Grand Canyon. This is a desert, with very little water. Instead, the Arches have been formed by a much slower, bit-by-bit process of erosion called weathering.

Although this is a desert, there is a little rain each spring—and a little ice every winter. In the process of weathering, water finds its way into the sandstone formations. The water very slowly eats away at the softer parts of the sandstone, leaving the harder parts standing. Weathering can take thousands of years, but in this way, all of these sandstone arches have been formed.

That small amount of water is also enough to support the life of the desert. There are bristlecone pines here that need very little water—and take two hundred years to grow. At night, the desert lizards come out, some of them a foot long. So do the foxes, jackrabbits, snakes, coyotes, and bobcats. In the higher places, there are also mountain lions. In the spring, the desert flowers bloom, forming a colorful carpet over the dry desert land of the Arches.

Assateague Island

Wild ponies run free on Assateague Island.

Assateague Island is famous for its wild ponies. They are meant to be forever free, protected in this mid-Atlantic seashore national park. A story is told about the ponies' ancestors. Those early ponies are said to have been on a Spanish galleon, a ship wrecked off the Maryland-Virginia coast hundreds of years ago. No one knows whether the story is really true. But the ponies are very real, and an important part of this wonderful place.

Assateague is a thirty-five-mile-long barrier island running alongside and protecting part of the Maryland-Virginia shore. Because it is narrow, only one-third of a mile to a mile wide, the sea always threatens to wash some parts of it away, as it did during a storm in 1933, which also cut away the island's connection to islands farther north.

Another, later storm made the current national park on the island possible. Until the 1960s, thousands of people lived on Assateague Island. But a hurricane in 1962 destroyed all but a few houses on the island. After that the island was reclaimed and protected as a national park.

Today, the southern end of Assateague Island is a wildlife refuge. In the large saltwater marshes there, the wild ponies can find food. Deer and raccoons also live in the marshes and pine woods on the island.

The long beaches of Assateague Island are also the home of thousands of shorebirds. And hundreds of thousands of birds stop at Assateague on their migration south and later back north every year. The island is one of the best places in the country for bird-watchers, who come to see pelicans, herons, ducks, geese, and scores of other kinds of shorebirds and water birds.

Auquittuq

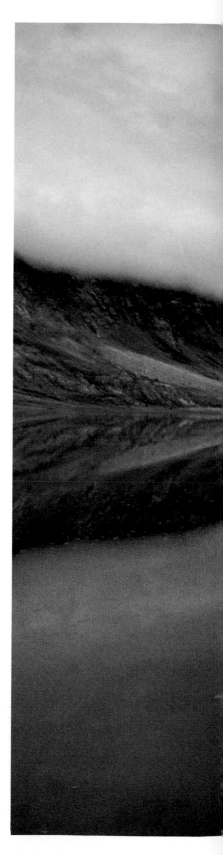

In the Inuit Eskimo language, *Auquittuq* means "the Place That Does Not Melt." It is a good name for this great park, far north on Canada's Atlantic coast. The park is on Baffin Island, between Greenland to the east and mainland Canada to the west.

For thousands of years, this has been Eskimo country. Vikings from Greenland may have explored Baffin Island a thousand years ago, but they probably did not stay long. English explorers, led by John Davis, came much later, a little over four hundred years ago. Baffin Island itself is named after William Baffin, an English navigator of the 1600s.

Here, on and above the Arctic Circle, is a land of everlasting ice and snow. At Auquittuq, granite mountains stand up to 7,000 feet high and are covered by the Penny Ice Cap, a mass of thick, deep, solid ice covering 2,200 square miles. Also among the mountains are huge glaciers. These are slow-moving "rivers" of ice as much as twenty miles long. Many of Auquittuq's long valleys were gouged out by glaciers over the course of hundreds of thousands of years. Cutting into the island's coast are deep and narrow bodies of water called fjords. Some of the fjords have steep walls as high as 3,000 feet—over half a mile.

Auquittuq is also a land of light and dark. In midwinter the sun never shines, and in midsummer the sun never sets. That is so in all the lands near the North Pole—and the South Pole, too. Because it is so near the North Pole, Auquittuq is also a very, very cold land. Its winter is long, while its summer is short and cool. In that kind of climate, and especially high in the mountains, not many plants or animals can live.

Yet in the short northern summer, the yellow arctic poppies and many other northern flowers do bloom. Then there are so many that the bare rocks turn into beautiful flowering rock gardens. And all year round, the land and sea do support a surprising number of creatures. On land, for example, there are polar bears, arctic foxes, and lemmings, which serve as prey for many of the larger animals. Among the sea creatures are Atlantic white whales and small whales called narwhals. There are also walruses, several kinds of seals, and the arctic char. The birds to be seen include snowy owls, ducks, Canada geese, ravens, gulls, and sometimes even rare falcons.

Ice-covered mountains are reflected in the water at Auquittuq.

Badlands

The Badlands, now bare and dry, was once an inland sea.

The Dakota Indians, who lived here long before the Europeans came, called this place *mako sica*. The French called it *les mauvises terres*. In both languages—and in ours—this is the Badlands. This part of South Dakota is a region of bare rock, with little vegetation or water. It is very hard country. In 1823, even the great trapper Jedediah Smith and his party ran out of water and nearly died trying to cross the Badlands.

Yet there is life here. The great buffalo herds are gone, but there are still antelope, coyote, mule deer, and many smaller grassland animals. Many kinds of birds are also found here, sometimes even a golden eagle. And in the spring, the prairie flowers blossom where you would think no flowers could possibly grow.

Long ago, there was much more life here. The land and the climate were very different then.

Eighty million years ago, this land was at the bottom of a sea. Later the sea bottom rose to become dry land. Thirty-five million years ago, the Badlands was a huge, level, marshy plain. Gradually that plain became the soft rock that is here today. This soft rock is slowly being worn away by wind and rain, forming the fantastic shapes, sharp ridges, and deep, narrow cuts that are the Badlands.

Signs of the earlier life of this place are there for all to see. There are abundant fossils throughout the Badlands. Here you can see the fossilized traces of such sea creatures as the huge sea turtles of long ago. You can also see the fossils of animals and birds that thrived when the Badlands became dry land—animals such as eagles, owls, tigers, and camels.

Big Sur

At Big Sur, the sea cuts the rock, leaving sea stacks.

Big Sur—the name is taken from the Spanish for "Big South"—is a fifty-mile-long stretch of California coastline, starting about one hundred miles south of San Francisco on the long coast road to Los Angeles. On that stretch of coastline, the Santa Lucia Mountains meet the Pacific Ocean, and the result is one of the wildest, most beautiful coastlines in the world. The road that twists and turns along the edge of those cliffs by the sea, California Route 1, is one of the world's best-known scenic routes.

The Big Sur country is a place of huge mountain headlands, rising up from waves that pound the shore. Offshore rock pinnacles called sea stacks mark where older headlands once stood, before the sea cut them away from the land. Farther out, you can see low rocky islands, once headlands, then sea stacks, soon to be cut away

further, and finally buried by the waves of the Pacific. This is a foggy, foggy coast, and on some days fog makes the road almost impassable. Indeed, mountains and fog made this part of the coast very hard to reach, so most of California's north-south traffic went inland, on the other side of the coastal mountains. The coast road was opened up only in the 1930s. Before then this was rough, unsettled country.

Big Sur's rocky coast provides shelter for many kinds of large sea creatures, including now-rare sea otters, pelicans, harbor seals, and sea lions. These live on kelp and smaller fish, while they themselves are hunted by the killer whales that also live here. Farther out to sea are the large gray whales that travel north to south along the coast in spring and fall.

7

Bryce Canyon

At Bryce Canyon, water-cut rocks make a fantasy world.

This is a place of fantastic rock formations, in many of the colors of the rainbow. To many visitors, the rock shapes look like people, animals, bridges, castles — whatever the imagination suggests. Bryce Canyon, in southern Utah, is a place where you can imagine you are seeing all the people and places of your dreams.

Actually, it is all a matter of soft rock and dripping water. For millions of years, rivers and streams have continuously cut sharp valleys, or canyons, into the ground. In the many smaller canyons that, together, are called Bryce Canyon,

the water has also eroded the strange rock formations that captivate the visitor. In the process, the rocks have been shaped and reshaped, over and over again. If you were a time traveler, and had come here a million years ago, you would have seen vastly different rock formations from those here now. And a million years from now, many will be very different again.

Five hundred years ago, this was Paiute Indian country. The Paiutes were still here when the first Spanish explorers came. Later, in the 1800s, American trappers came here, too. They took so many beavers that there were finally no more. Later, Mormon settlers came, moving west to find a place to practice their religion.

The beavers are gone, but there are still bobcats, owls, hawks, foxes, and scores of other kinds of animals and birds in Bryce Canyon. There are also a great number of trees, flowers, and grasses. And the rock formations remain, in all their fantastic, ever-changing sizes, shapes, and colors.

Cape Breton

Some of the earliest European settlers came to beautiful Cape Breton.

You can stand high on the mountainous tip of Cape Breton, look far out across the North Atlantic, and imagine that Europe is just over the horizon. Canada's Cape Breton Island is the most northern part of Nova Scotia.

Some of the earliest Europeans to visit Cape Breton, long before the French settled here, were probably Basques from Spain. They fished in North Atlantic waters even before Columbus came to America. Norse Vikings from Scandinavia had settled Iceland and Greenland five hundred years before Columbus, and may have visited Cape Breton, too.

But the Basques and others did not settle on Cape Breton. Settlement came only after Columbus. Explorers such as John Cabot and Jacques Cartier came first. They were quickly followed by soldiers, trappers, traders, priests, settlers, and many others. Cartier sailed south past Cape Breton, into the St. Lawrence River, and on into what would become Canada. He claimed what is now Nova Scotia for France,

Today visitors by the thousands follow Cape Breton's old Cabot Trail.

calling it Acadia. The French knew Cape Breton Island as the *Isle Royale,* or the "Royal Island." Later, under British rule, Acadia was renamed Nova Scotia, and the island was renamed Cape Breton. In the 1700s, the French and the British battled for control of North America in the long series of wars that ended with the French and Indian War. The French built the huge fortress of Louisbourg on the southeast coast of Cape Breton Island. The British took it, and then moved on to take Quebec. With that, they ended the war.

Cape Breton is hilly, rough country, with mountains well over a thousand feet high. Much of its great beauty is in those mountains, which in many places drop right down into the wild Atlantic Ocean. Cape Breton Highlands National Park covers almost four hundred square miles of high, rugged country. In these high-lands away from the sea, bears live, and huge flocks of seabirds nest along the rocky coast. Atlantic salmon run in the highland streams and are much prized by Canadian and American fishermen.

Cape Breton is also cold country, although the land is warmed to some extent in winter by the Atlantic's Gulf Stream, that huge current of warmer water that flows north from Florida along the coast of North America. But this is still harsh country. The trees, mostly northern pines, grow leaning toward the land and away from the sea, pushed that way by the cold wind that blows in off the Atlantic. The Cabot Trail, a highway that runs for 184 miles around the whole northern end of Cape Breton Island, offers views of mountains, sea, and wide, wide sky, which make it one of the most beautiful roads in the world.

Cape Cod

High on Cape Cod's sand dunes is its famous lighthouse.

Here are miles and miles of graceful sand dunes facing the stormy North Atlantic. The ocean's waves and winds keep on cutting away at the dunes in some places. They carry away sand to build more dunes on another part of the shore. There are gulls overhead, clams on the sandy beaches, and whales out to sea. This is Cape Cod National Seashore, in southern Massachusetts, a long, narrow arm of land sticking out into the sea.

The Pilgrims actually landed at Cape Cod first, before going on to Plymouth, where they finally settled. On November 11, 1620, the *Mayflower* dropped anchor in the harbor at the tip of Cape Cod, at what is now Provincetown. The ship stayed there for five weeks before the colonists decided to move on.

The never-ending action of the ocean has changed the face of Cape Cod many times since Pilgrim days. But there is much the same feel of huge blue sky, wind, sand, birds, and ocean. Cape Cod is a paradise for bird-watchers, beach walkers, and naturalists. Up from the dunes on the beach are salt marshes and then fields of heather. In places, there are stands of white cedar, some dating back to Pilgrim times. A little inland are cranberry bogs, strikingly red in the autumn.

Bird-watchers can see scores of different kinds of birds here. Some species live here all year long. Others pass through on their spring and fall journeys north and south, like the terns that fly all the way to southern seas and back every year. In the fall, especially, huge flocks of water birds gather — sandpipers, plovers, killdeers, the rare eagle, and thousands and thousands of sea gulls. At Cape Cod, you can see them all.

Cape Hatteras

Peaceful-looking Cape Hatteras is battered by year-round Atlantic storms.

Cape Hatteras has the tallest lighthouse on the whole Atlantic coast of the United States. From here, on a clear day, you can see far out to sea, to where the blue sky and the equally blue sea meet. On that kind of day, it is often hard to see where the sea ends and the sky begins — or to know whether a speck on the horizon is a ship on the water or a plane in the air.

Cape Hatteras National Seashore is a piece of North Carolina's Outer Banks. The Outer Banks is a chain of very narrow barrier islands stretching almost two hundred miles along the shore of North Carolina. These are beautiful, narrow, low, sandy islands — wonderful places for bird-watchers and, in summer, for beach-going vacationers. In the sea, there are large marlin and tuna, and lots of bass, bluefish, and mackerel. On land, there are the wild Ocracoke ponies, a must for all visitors to see.

But this is also the wildest, stormiest piece of coastline on the Atlantic coast. At Cape Hatteras, the Gulf Stream, a great warm current flowing north in the Atlantic, meets colder currents along the shore. The clash of air masses spurs many storms. Most Atlantic storms headed for the mainland hit this exposed part of the coast — and any ships sailing nearby — terribly hard. Off this coast lie thousands of sunken wrecks, from tiny sailing ships dating back nearly to Columbus to the big steamships of modern times. That is why the sea off Cape Hatteras has long been known as the Graveyard of the Atlantic.

Carlsbad Caverns

Bats first led settlers to explore the enormous Carlsbad Caverns.

Millions of bats, pouring out of a big hole in the side of a mountain every evening and returning home by sunrise—that is what led New Mexico settlers to discover Carlsbad Caverns in the 1800s.

At first, people went into the caverns only as far as the big Bat Cave. There they mined guano —bat droppings used as fertilizer. But in 1901, cave explorer Jim White went much farther in. He found that Carlsbad was a huge, deep set of connected caves, with many very beautiful and striking features. By now, miles of caves have been explored, some of them over one thousand feet deep. And now millions of people visit such attractions as the huge Big Room, 285 feet high.

Millions of years ago, a thick reef of land stood beside an inland sea here. Later, the reef turned to limestone, and the land rose up out of the sea. Then rain and running water began to carve the big caves in the soft limestone. What happens in all such limestone caves is that water drips very slowly from the ceiling of the caverns. The water mixes with minerals in the limestone to form an acid, which eats away the limestone and forms the great caves. But the water-and-mineral mixture also forms strange new shapes in the caverns. As it drips from above, it builds up the long, colorful rocks called stalactites that look like icicles hanging from the ceiling. Underneath them, the same, dripping water gradually forms the upside-down icicles called stalagmites, rising from the cavern floor. Water slowly flowing down the sides of the caverns builds up what looks like sheets of ice but are really a kind of stone called flowstone. The beautiful colors in the rocks are caused by the minerals in the dripping water. Iron makes the stone a rusty red, for example, and copper makes it a brilliant green.

Carlsbad Caverns has many thousands of unusual and beautiful rock formations, from very small ones that look like pearls and soda straws to such big forms as the Temple of the Sun and the Giant Dome.

Columbia Icefield

The Icefields Parkway runs alongside the Athabaska Glacier.

The Columbia Icefield is a huge mass of ice that never fully melts. It covers four hundred square miles of land, high in Canada's Rocky Mountains, and in many places is as much as thirty-three hundred feet thick.

Some icefields in far northern Canada and Alaska are much larger. But the Columbia Icefield is both very large and easy to reach. It lies near the resort towns of Banff and Jasper, in Canada's Alberta province. Thousands of people visit Banff and Jasper every year to climb and to study scientifically the massive icefield. The Columbia Icefield is made up of not just one but about thirty glaciers. Each glacier is a mass of ice—really a "river" of ice—that is moving very slowly from the top of the mountains down toward the valleys. As the weather and climate change, these glaciers sometimes get larger and reach farther down into the valleys, and sometimes grow smaller and retreat up the hillsides. Two of the Columbia Icefield's largest glaciers are the Athabaska and Saskatchewan glaciers. The Athabaska is especially easy to reach and climb, because a highway called the Icefields Parkway runs alongside it.

The Columbia Icefield is located among mountains 10,000 to 12,000 feet high. It sits directly on the Continental Divide—the big ridge that runs most of the length of the Rockies and that actually divides the waters of the continent. From the Continental Divide, water flowing west begins its journey of 1,200 miles into the Columbia River system and finally out to the Pacific. Water flowing north begins its trip of 2,500 miles through the Athabaska and Mackenzie rivers to the Arctic Ocean. Water moving east flows 1,600 miles to Hudson Bay, by way of the North Saskatchewan River. That is why the Columbia Icefield has often been called the Mother of Rivers.

14

Crater Lake

High atop the Cascade Mountains of Oregon lies the very blue, very deep, and very beautiful Crater Lake. The water in this mountain lake is some of the clearest and cleanest in the world. But that is only a small part of the reason the water is so blue. The deep blue color is primarily due to the lake's being so deep. At 1,932 feet, it is the deepest lake in the United States. At that depth, most of the many colors in the sun's rays are caught and held. What is left are the blue rays that are reflected back up through the clean, clear water.

A huge volcano erupted here between sixty-five hundred and seven thousand years ago. Where Crater Lake now sits, there once stood the peak of a high volcanic mountain, called Mount Mazama. The volcano let go with a powerful explosion—so strong that it cracked the cone on top of the mountain. The whole mountain then collapsed inward, creating the huge crater that is here today. The crater gradually filled with rainwater, melted ice, and snow, creating Crater Lake.

There is evidence that early Americans were living here when Mount Mazama exploded. Some of them may have been the ancestors of the Klamath tribe, which inhabited the area until the 1850s. In 1853, Crater Lake was first explored by John Wesley Hillman, who was prospecting for gold in these mountains. Since 1902, blue and beautiful Crater Lake has been protected as a national park.

Deep, blue Crater Lake lies in the ruins of an old dead volcano.

Death Valley

The deep, hot, dry valley called Death Valley is in southern California. It is about 140 miles long, 5 to 15 miles wide, and hemmed in by mountain ranges on both sides. The valley does have some springs, but mostly it is as dry a desert as can be found in North America. Death Valley gets an average of less than two inches of rain every year. In summer, temperatures often reach as high as 134 degrees Fahrenheit. It is also the lowest place in North America—in one spot 282 feet below sea level.

This forbidding place is called Death Valley because that is just what it was for some people, back in the days when many Americans headed west during the California gold rush. In 1849, a party of pioneers lost their way and were trapped in Death Valley without enough water. Those who lived to tell the story got out by climbing the ten-thousand-foot-high mountains to the west. But some never got out at all. However, these pioneers were not the first people in the valley. Long before their time, the Indian peoples of the Southwest had lived in and around Death Valley.

Once, thousands of years ago, the valley had plenty of water. That was a time when melting glaciers left a whole string of lakes in what is now the California desert. The footprints—now turned into stone—of such animals as camels, water birds, and antelopes have been found in Death Valley.

All this makes it sound like a place no one would like to visit. But part of Death Valley is also a national monument, and for very good reasons. Not only is it a wonder in its starkness, but sometimes, in the spring, in a year when there has been a little more rainfall than usual, the whole desert seems to come alive with blooming flowers. It does not happen often—maybe every five to ten years—but when it does, it is something to remember for a lifetime.

In different ways, Death Valley is always beautiful and unusual. There is much red sandstone here. Canyon walls full of minerals shine with all the colors of the rainbow in the hot desert sun. There are the creatures and plants of the desert, too. Death Valley has a dozen different kinds of animals, including jackrabbits, bighorn sheep, and foxes. If you watch closely, you can also see lizards and horned toads. There are snakes, too, including rattlesnakes. In the air you can see many kinds of birds, such as quails, meadowlarks, and mourning doves. The desert is the home of many different kinds of cactus plants. Up in the mountains surrounding the valley are such trees as bristlecone pines, junipers, and Rocky Mountain maples. In truth, Death Valley is full of life, for those who look hard enough.

Living creatures are hard to find in the aptly named Death Valley.

Everglades

In the early 1800s, this great swamp in South Florida was the refuge of the Seminole Indians. No army could follow and find them in the Everglades. They lived in the swamp with their runaway-slave allies and were never defeated.

Today, the Everglades is a refuge of a different kind. Now it is a great nature preserve. It is the land of the alligator, the saw-grass sea, the mangrove forest, and of many, many kinds of water birds. The Everglades is full of the most colorful, beautiful water birds in North America.

Some water birds live here all year, while others pass through on their yearly trips north and south along the Atlantic coast. One of them is the anhinga, a fishing bird also called the snakebird, because of its long neck. The anhinga has a long, sharp beak, and uses its neck and beak as a spear to catch fish in the water. In the mangrove forests of the Everglades live the bright pink and very beautiful birds called roseate spoonbills. There are also several kinds of herons, white ibises, pelicans, bald eagles, terns, gulls, cormorants, and many, many more. The Everglades is one of the best bird-watching places in the world.

The Everglades is a watery tropical jungle. A sea of ten-foot-high saw grass grows out of the soft, rich mud bottom of the swamp, and covers most of it. But large areas are raised just a few inches above the level of the water in the swamp. On that raised land, you can see mahogany trees, royal palms, silver palms, mangroves, buttonwoods, palmettos, cypresses, and many other tropical trees seldom found in the United States.

Many creatures of land and water live in the Everglades, too. The white-tailed deer here cannot eat the tough upper ends of the saw grass, but they uproot the saw grass and eat the softer bottom ends. The raccoons are creatures of the night, and you may not see them—but they are always there. You will hear and see some of the legion of frogs, and probably see some of the many turtles here. You will certainly see some of the great fifteen-foot-long alligators that roam the swamp, and hear the thump of their tails from a long way off. The twenty or so different kinds of snakes here are harder to spot, but coral snakes, water moccasins, diamondback rattlers, blacksnakes, king snakes, and many more thrive in the Everglades. There are also otters, gray foxes, opossums, and even a few panthers in the swamp.

An alligator suns himself in Florida's Everglades.

Glacier Bay

Huge chunks of Muir Glacier break off—or calve—into the sea at Glacier Bay.

In Alaska's Glacier Bay, the huge glaciers go right down to the sea. Sometimes the ice breaks off the face of the glaciers in chunks hundreds of feet wide—with a roar that can be heard for miles.

Almost two hundred years ago, British sailor George Vancouver explored the western coast of North America. The Canadian city of Vancouver is named after him. Along the coast of Alaska, he passed a huge, solid wall of ice, three thousand feet thick, at what is now Glacier Bay. But he saw no bay there at all. Later, the climate warmed up just a little, and some of the glaciers began to melt back, exposing the bay that had been there all the time. By 1879, the great wilderness explorer and naturalist John Muir found Glacier Bay. He was deeply moved by the beauty of this place.

The most striking of all the glaciers here is Muir Glacier, named after John Muir. It is a truly immense glacier, with a solid ice face two miles wide and over 250 feet high. Gradually Muir Glacier is becoming shorter, for big chunks of ice break off as the end of the glacier moves back, away from the sea. The glacier has pulled back many miles since John Muir first saw it.

A great number of sea and land creatures live in and around Glacier Bay. In the sea there are many porpoises, seals, and sea lions; large colonies of humpback whales in summer; and even some big killer whales. Here, too, are millions of salmon that are born in the streams feeding the bay. On land there are three kinds of big bears—the Alaska brown bear, the grizzly, and the black bear. Wolves, deer, beavers, lynxes, foxes, and mountain goats roam the shores of the bay, and bald eagles, loons, and great blue herons rule the skies above. Glacier Bay is one of the finest northern wildlife preserves in the world.

Glacier National Park

The glacier-covered Montana peaks were once at the bottom of the sea.

Glacier National Park is named after the rivers of ice that formed much of this land, starting a million years ago. The ice retreated then, but came back ten thousand years ago, and then again four thousand years ago. The park still holds about sixty small glaciers.

This is the land of the bighorn sheep, which can walk easily and gracefully along the sides of mountains, where no human being can possibly go. This high mountain country in northern Montana is also inhabited by the grizzly bear, black bear, elk, moose, beaver, otter, badger, and many more species. You can see golden eagles here, too, along with bald eagles, grouses, ptarmigans, thrushes, jays, and scores of other birds.

Long ago—hundreds of millions of years ago —this land was the bottom of a sea. Over its long history, it was submerged by seawater again and again. Each time, a layer of mud and sand formed on the seafloor. Later it hardened into rock. Much later, strong forces deep within the earth pushed the land upward, forming the high Rocky Mountains, which run through western North America from Canada to Mexico. At Glacier National Park, high in the mountains, you can see many of these rocks that were once part of the seafloor.

Glacier National Park is on the Canadian border. Across the border, in Canada, lies Waterton Lakes National Park. The two parks together form Waterton-Glacier International Peace Park. They honor almost two centuries of peace between the United States and Canada.

Grand Canyon

The huge, deep valley called Grand Canyon is one of the most spectacular natural wonders of the world. Grand Canyon runs 217 miles through the high tableland, or plateau, that forms northern Arizona. At its bottom is the twisting Colorado River. Over millions of years the river has cut the canyon a mile deep into the earth.

Although it is dangerous, some people travel through the canyon by boat on the river. However, most people visit Grand Canyon on foot, descending into the canyon from one of the rims. It is a long, hard climb, but it is well worth it. The rock formations display beautiful colors and reveal traces of early life. Several times in its long history, the land into which the canyon is cut was covered by the sea. The layers of material that settled to the bottom of that sea are what contain glimpses of the past, in hardened deposits called fossils. Near the top of Grand Canyon, fossil seashells, sponges, and coral formations are set in limestone. Farther down, you can see the fossil tracks of dinosaurs and sea animals, and traces of the plants that grew at that time. Even farther down, there are traces of very early tiny beings called trilobites. There, too, are some of the earliest seashells on earth. All the way down, there is only rock. Some of this rock is two billion years old, going far back into the early life of the planet.

At first look, Grand Canyon appears to be mostly bare red rock and desert. But in truth it is populated by a tremendous amount of wildlife. Along the swift-flowing river at the bottom are beavers, otters, ducks, blue herons, and many other animals. Higher up are a great variety of birds, from huge golden eagles to tiny hummingbirds. Higher up, still, are the mountain meadows and the ponderosa pine forests that cover both rims.

People have lived in Grand Canyon for a long time. Far down in the canyon you can see Indian stone carvings four thousand years old. The Anasazi people—their name means "the Old Ones"—lived here for hundreds of years. They were here long before the Vikings came to Greenland, and many hundreds of years before Columbus came to America.

The first Spanish explorers of the Southwest were led to Grand Canyon in 1540 by Hopi Indian guides. And Indians are here yet. Many Hopis, Navajos, and Havasupais live and work in and near Grand Canyon. In fact, a small Havasupai reservation is located near the northern end of the canyon. Today, Grand Canyon is one of the most popular of America's national parks, with over a million visitors every year.

As the river cuts the Grand Canyon, it travels farther back in earth's history.

Great Sand Dunes

Wind has piled up these Great Sand Dunes in Colorado.

In southern Colorado there lies a big desert valley with a ten-mile stretch of huge sand dunes. Some of the dunes are as much as eight hundred feet high. The dunes are in the San Luis Valley and back up against a great two-mile-high, snowcapped mountain range called the Sangre de Cristo ("Blood of Christ") Mountains.

These are Spanish names, for Spanish explorers and settlers moving north from Mexico were the first Europeans to come here. But long before the Spanish came, this was Indian country. It was the land of the Ute, Apache, Cheyenne, and Comanche. Later, it became the land of the American "mountain men" and explorers, like Zebulon Pike and Kit Carson. Later still, the Sangre de Cristo Mountains sheltered such famous Apache warriors as Cochise and Geronimo in their long wars against the American army.

What made these dunes—and keeps on making them—is a combination of wind, desert, and mountains. The wind here almost always blows from the south, toward the mountains, picking up sand from the desert floor as it goes. As the wind rises to go over the mountains it drops the heavy sand, thereby forming the big dunes along the sides of the mountains. Once in a while, the wind does shift, moving the sand a little in the other direction. But soon the wind shifts back to the south again, and the sand is pinned against the mountains in these great dunes.

These are the biggest desert sand dunes in North America. Their size, the nearby mountains, and the sharpness of the sun and shadows in the desert air make the Great Sand Dunes a wonderful place for taking pictures. And many photographers have come from far away to do just that.

Hawaii Volcanoes

The island of Hawaii has five huge volcanoes. Actually, the whole island is made up of the joined tops of all the volcanoes. These volcanoes rise all the way from the floor of the Pacific Ocean up to almost fifteen thousand feet above sea level. The highest of them, Mauna Loa, is thirty thousand feet high, measuring from the seafloor. That makes it the largest mountain in the world, even larger than Mount Everest, although Mount Everest is measured from sea level.

Three of the five volcanoes here are quiet now. But Mauna Loa and Kilauea are two of the most active volcanoes in the world. They are the prime attractions in the Hawaii Volcanoes National Park. During an eruption in 1959, Kilauea shot a fountain of hot lava nineteen hundred feet high into the air. During eruptions, lava some-times flows down the sides of the mountains at speeds of twenty-five miles an hour. And it may flow for as far as twenty miles before it begins to harden into rock. Sometimes, as during an eruption in 1986, the lava reaches the sea, causing the water to boil.

At Mauna Loa, you can drive and climb to the top of the volcano and look over the rim into the three-mile-wide crater. There you can see the huge pool of molten lava that oozes up from a hot spot in the earth's crust, as much as thirty-five miles deep. When pressure inside the earth builds up, the volcano erupts, throwing a big pool of lava high into the air, and pushing floods of lava over and through the sides of the crater. We can expect these active volcanoes to erupt again and again during our lifetimes.

Red-hot lava from Kilauea Volcano flows downhill toward the sea.

Howe Caverns

Dripping water and limestone have created Howe Caverns' amazing formations.

Deep underground in central New York State's Schoharie Valley lies one of America's most colorful, interesting sets of caverns. A 156-foot-deep elevator takes visitors down into Howe Caverns. That is as deep as a seventeen-story building is tall. The caverns are named after Lester Howe, who explored them in 1842.

The wonderful colors and shapes here were formed by a combination of slowly dripping water, colored minerals in that water, and the slow wearing away of stone. That is what creates all such caverns.

Millions of years ago, this land lay under an arm of the Atlantic Ocean. Over a very long time, the sea bottom was covered by seashells and other bits of material left there by the shellfish and other creatures of the sea. Gradually, a bed of such material built up, hundreds of feet thick. Later, it all pressed together and fi-

nally turned into limestone.

Later yet, the sea bottom rose up out of the water and became dry land. Then the rains began to wear away at the soft limestone. Gradually they made the deep underground streams and caves that today are Howe Caverns.

That wearing away of the limestone by water is still happening far underground here. In the process, beautiful and unusual stalactites, stalagmites, flowstone, and other such shapes continue to form. (For more about these formations, see Carlsbad Caverns entry on p. 13)

At Howe Caverns, the stones have worn into all kinds of fantastic shapes. One of them looks like an old witch, another like a Chinese pagoda, and still another like a great pipe organ. Caverns are always fascinating places to see, and Howe Caverns is one of the most fascinating of all.

Hudson River Palisades

English navigator Henry Hudson and his Dutch crew saw the Hudson River Palisades in 1609 as they sailed their ship, the *Half Moon*, north on what was later to be named the Hudson River in his honor. The palisades are a line of steep, rocky cliffs, 350 to 550 feet high, on the west side of the Hudson River, running 48 miles from Jersey City, New Jersey, to Pomona, New York. They are so named because they look very much like a huge fence of stakes, called a palisade. And their appearance, in turn, is a result of the way they were formed.

Two hundred million years ago, there was tremendous volcanic activity here and all along the eastern edge of the Appalachian Mountains. That activity deposited enormous amounts of sandstone and other soft rocks along the west bank of the Hudson. It also pushed up great amounts of molten lava, which cooled to form extremely hard basalt in dark vertical strips called traprock. Much later, glaciers scoured the area, pushing much of the soft sandstone away, and exposing the high columns of hard traprock underneath. These are the palisades we see today.

The extraordinary beauty of the palisades has inspired generations of American painters, including some of the great painters of the Hudson River School. The palisades were also some of the first massive land formations seen by tens of millions of immigrants, going north on the Hudson to Albany, and from there west into North America. The Hudson River itself, though only 315 miles long, has always been one of the main pathways into North America, and one of America's great historic rivers.

The striking Palisades inspired many of the Hudson River School painters.

Joshua Tree National Monument

Rare Joshua trees—relatives of the lily—form a unique California forest.

In southern California, near Riverside, there is a place of desert, mountain, and forest—but a very unusual kind of forest. The desert is the Mojave, very dry and very hot. The mountains are the Little San Bernardino Mountains. They stand in the shadow of mountains over twice as high, stretching up into the High Sierras to the north. From the five-thousand-foot-high spot called Salton View, you can see California's Imperial Valley, the mountain ranges, and sometimes all the way south into Mexico.

The very unusual forest there is a Joshua tree forest. This is the finest stand of these rare trees anywhere in the world. To preserve them, this area has been set aside as a national monument since 1936.

Joshua trees are sometimes mistaken for cactuses. That is because they have the dry, spiny look shared by so many desert plants. But they are really a kind of yucca, and yuccas are part of the lily family. So all members of the lily family are not like the slim, delicate lilies found in some gardens. These members of the lily family grow up to forty feet high, and some are over ten feet around. In the spring, when they bloom, masses of white flowers hang from the ends of their branches. Then you can see that they are indeed something like giant lilies.

Katmai Volcano

The cone of Mount Katmai blew off in a volcanic eruption in 1912.

In June of 1912, in southern Alaska, a huge volcanic mountain called Mount Katmai exploded. The explosion was so powerful that it could be felt and heard many hundreds of miles away. Nearby Kodiak Island was covered with volcanic ash. More volcanic ash filled the sky—so much that the brightness of the sun was dimmed for months afterward, all around the northern half of the world. The once-green valley next to the volcano became more like a valley on the moon. Thousands of volcanic holes puffed lava and smoke into the air. Most of those volcanic holes have stopped smoking now. But to this day that valley is called the Valley of Ten Thousand Smokes.

At the same time, Mount Katmai collapsed—just as Mount Mazama in Oregon had collapsed to form Crater Lake thousands of years earlier.

Here, too, only the big, empty crater was left, after the lava ran out of the center of the mountain. And here, too, what then formed was a deep, blue lake. (The one at Katmai is about half the size of Crater Lake.)

Katmai is only one of many such volcanoes in this part of North America. A whole range of volcanoes covers about eighty miles of the Alaska coast. This is also one of Alaska's biggest nature preserves, like Glacier Bay farther south. The Alaska brown bear, which is the world's biggest kind of bear, lives here. Some of these bears weigh as much as fifteen hundred pounds and stand ten feet tall. At Katmai you can also see wolves, caribous, beavers, ptarmigans, thrushes, whistling swans, geese, and dozens of other kinds of animals and birds.

Lake Louise

High in the Canadian Rockies lies one of the most beautiful mountain lakes in North America —or for that matter, in the world. It is Lake Louise, at Banff National Park, in the province of Alberta.

Higher still is the Victoria Glacier, a huge mass of ice sitting on the ten-thousand-foot-high mountain slopes above Lake Louise. The melting and runoff from the glacier constantly feeds and refreshes the cool, clear, blue water of the lake. Mountains, glacier, lake, and sky have made this one of the most popular places in Canada.

So, too, is the rest of Banff National Park. This is Canada's first national park, dating back to 1885. At that time, ten square miles of hot mineral springs and pools were set aside by the Canadian government—much as the hot springs at Yellowstone, in the United States, had been set aside only thirteen years earlier. Since then, though, Banff National Park has grown a great deal. Now it covers over 2,500 square miles and runs for about 75 miles along the eastern slope of the Canadian Rockies. The park includes many mountain peaks 10,000 to 12,000 feet high, and dozens of mountain lakes, hot springs, and pools. At the north end of the park is the beginning of the massive Columbia Icefield, with its many glaciers.

Lake Louise and Banff have much wildlife, too. Visitors can see elk, deer, grizzly bear, black bear, moose, mountain sheep, and many other kinds of animals. But they are well advised to stay away from the bears, who may be friendly, but are also large, strong, and sometimes all too eager to be fed.

Beautiful Lake Louise is one of Banff National Park's main attractions.

Mississippi River

Below cliffs near St. Louis, barges move up the mighty Mississippi.

In the Ojibway Indian language, *Missi Sipi* means "Great River." It is certainly that. The mighty Mississippi is by far the greatest river in North America. Actually, the Mississippi River system is far more than a single river. It is really a whole network of rivers in the center of the continent. Those rivers gather water from over a million square miles of land between the Rocky Mountains and the Appalachian Mountains and pour it into the Gulf of Mexico.

The three biggest rivers in the system are the Missouri, the Ohio, and the Mississippi itself. The Missouri starts far out west, in the Rockies, and flows through the western plains, picking up so much mud and silt on the way that it has long been called the Big Muddy. It flows past such major cities as Omaha and Kansas City before joining the Mississippi at St. Louis. The Ohio starts to the east, in the Appalachian Mountains. It flows past such cities as Cincinnati and Louisville to join the Mississippi at Cairo, Illinois. Having drawn water from these

two—and many smaller rivers, too—the Mississippi then flows out past New Orleans into the Gulf of Mexico.

Along the way, the river passes through much of America and its history. This is the river of the great Hopewell Indian culture, which was here long before the Europeans came. The huge Hopewell burial mounds can still be seen along the river at Cahokia, Illinois, and many other places. The Mississippi is also the river of steamboating days, the river Mark Twain loved and wrote about. In those days all the grain and cotton of America's Midwest and Mid-South floated down the river to New Orleans, and long lines of barges pulled by tugboats still carry all the products of America's heartland down the river. Abe Lincoln traveled on the Mississippi when he was a young man. He sent Ulysses Grant and a whole Union army to take Vicksburg on the river during the Civil War. This is the river of America's pioneers, heroes, soldiers, and farmers—truly our Great River.

Mount Logan

Hardy climbers have carved out a path over wintry Mount Logan's ice pack.

From way up on Mount Logan, in Canada's far Northwest, you can see hundreds of square miles of ice fields, glaciers, and mountain ranges. This is a big, wild land—a country of ice and snow, and of many great, jagged peaks towering high over the frozen ice pack below.

At over nineteen thousand feet, Mount Logan is Canada's highest mountain. It is part of Canada's Kluane National Park, in the Yukon Territory, near the Alaska border. It is also one of the highest mountains in North America. It is far higher than those of the Rockies, and many of the mountains around Mount Logan in the St. Elias range are nearly as tall, over fifteen thousand feet high.

In this wild country, a great many kinds of birds and animals live and flourish. Golden eagles, bald eagles, and peregrine falcons are hard to find farther south, but they are found here. So are arctic terns, mountain bluebirds, rock ptarmigans, and scores of other kinds of birds. Actually, over 150 kinds of birds have been seen in Kluane Park.

You can also see many kinds of animals that are very rare elsewhere. Among them are thousands of Dall sheep, many mountain goats, grizzly bears and black bears, herds of caribous, and even the largest kind of moose found in North America. This is one of the last big places on earth that so many birds and animals can all live together, free and wild.

People have been here for a long time, too. This area is on the great human migration route from Asia to the Americas. As long as thirty thousand years ago, people may have lived here. We know that people were certainly here as long as ten thousand years ago. They came across what was then dry land between Asia and Alaska, traveled right on into this country, and then moved south.

Mount McKinley

Long before the Europeans came, this huge mountain was known to the Indians as *Denali*. The name means "the Big One"—and it is. Mount McKinley, in the Alaska Range, is the highest mountain in North America. Its summit, always crowned with ice, is 20,320 feet above sea level. That is not nearly as tall as some of the world's highest mountains, such as Mount Everest. But from the ground, Mount McKinley looks as high as the highest mountain in the world. That is because mountains like Everest rise up from much higher ground to begin with. The distance between the bottom and the top of Mount McKinley is much like the distance between the bottom and the top of Mount Everest, if one were to place them side by side.

Mount McKinley is in southern Alaska, in very cold country. At its peak, it is one of the coldest places in the world, with temperatures sometimes falling as low as fifty degrees below zero Fahrenheit. Two-thirds of the mountain is always covered with snow, and many huge glaciers flow slowly down its slopes. One of

Alaska's Mount McKinley is the tallest peak in North America.

them, the Muldrow Glacier, is thirty-five miles long.

Mount McKinley is part of Denali National Park, which comprises almost two million acres of unspoiled mountains, glaciers, and forests. In spite of the climate, there is a tremendous amount of life here. You can see thousands of caribous, roaming in large herds. The bighorn Dall mountain sheep are here, too—and the timber wolves who prey on them. There are many grizzly bears, who wake up every spring and come out hungry. The largest animal here is the Alaska moose. It can weigh up to seventeen hundred pounds, with antlers spreading as much as five feet across.

You will not see any green things growing here for most of the year, but in the very short warm season, the frozen ground here—the tundra—thaws just a few inches down. Then the whole ground becomes a mass of color—of green grasses, budding trees, and such colorful flowers as the bright red arctic poppy.

Mount McKinley's snowy peak offers dramatic lights and shadows.

Mount St. Helens

In earlier times, people were often taken by surprise when volcanoes erupted. Some of the worst disasters in history have happened that way. The old Roman city of Pompeii was buried during an eruption, and all its people with it.

Today, scientists can tell us when volcanoes are likely to erupt. Such an early warning can save thousands of lives. But it is still very hard to know how strong an eruption will be.

Mount St. Helens, part of the Cascade Range in Washington State, is an active volcano. As volcanos go, it is young. It first started erupting about forty thousand years ago. English captain George Vancouver was the first European to see its great snowcapped cone. He had come north exploring the Pacific Coast in 1792. Mount St. Helens had erupted many times by then. Before this century, its last eruption was in 1857. Scientists predicted that it would erupt again before the year 2000.

It did, in May 1980—and with a huge explosion. There was early warning, from earthquakes that began almost two months earlier. So the people living nearby had a chance to leave before the disaster happened. But when it did come, it was a very powerful eruption.

The eruption began with an earthquake that started a huge avalanche of rocks, snow, and ice from the side of the mountain. That avalanche released an even more powerful and fiery explosion across the land. A hot blast, traveling 250 miles an hour, swept north, killing almost all plants and animals for six miles. The explosion

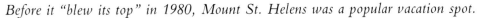

Before it "blew its top" in 1980, Mount St. Helens was a popular vacation spot.

blew down forests twenty miles away. It also killed some scientists who were there to study the volcano, from what they thought would be a fairly safe distance. The explosion could be heard hundreds of miles away.

Within fifteen minutes, the eruption blew a huge cloud of volcanic ash fifteen miles high. The ash formed a cloud that blocked out all sunlight in places over one hundred miles away, and some of the ash fell to earth nearly one thousand miles away. Within a month, the ash cloud from Mount St. Helens had traveled all the way around the world. This was one of the most powerful eruptions in modern times. The 1912 eruption of Mount Katmai in Alaska, though, was many times more powerful. And the volcanic eruption that made Crater Lake, in Oregon, about forty-seven hundred years ago, was even stronger.

Mount St. Helens erupted again and again in the following months, though not as violently as the first time. It has settled down now, but no one knows for how long. This is a young, very active, powerful volcano. The only sure thing is that it will erupt again.

After the eruption, the cone was gone and black ash covered the ground.

Niagara Falls

A boat takes visitors to where the Niagara Falls crashes down.

Visitors come to Niagara Falls from all over the world. They are struck most by the great power of the water pouring over the falls. From a short distance upstream, the Niagara River just looks very fast and smooth. Closer to the falls, you hear the noise of the water as it breaks over the lip of the falls, and you see the mist rising from below. Close up, the sheer power and roar of the whole Niagara River, pouring over the falls, is enough to take your breath away. In early times, before the noise created by industry and cars, people could hear the roar of the falls as much as twenty-five miles away. If you visit the falls in the warmer months, you can take a boat ride that moves in close to the mist at the foot of Niagara Falls. You can also go down through a tunnel to a spot right behind the crashing water.

Actually, there are two waterfalls here. The Niagara River is right on the border between the United States and Canada, and it splits in two just before the falls. Most of the water then pours over Canada's Horseshoe Falls, so named because they are shaped in a semicircle, like a horseshoe. At almost half a mile wide, the Horseshoe Falls are over twice as wide as the much-less-powerful American Falls beside them.

Both waterfalls seem to be forever smashing the rocks they tumble over — and that is just what is happening. The Niagara River here flows over limestone. The action of the water under the falls causes the rock below the top to wear away. When it does, the limestone on the top breaks away. Visitors can sometimes actually see large chunks of rock breaking off, with a

Canada's Horseshoe Falls is the larger of the two falls at Niagara.

thunderous roar of their own. Because of this, the lips of both waterfalls are continually moving backward a little. In the ten thousand years that the falls have existed, they have moved over six miles upstream.

Niagara Falls is one of the most-visited places in North America. At 185 to 190 feet high, they are not the highest falls in the world. Some falls elsewhere are up to twenty times as high. They are not even the most powerful falls in the world, though they are certainly very powerful. But they surely are by far the most popular waterfalls in the world—and have been for almost a century and a half.

That is partly because the falls are easy to get to. Furthermore, the falls drew a lot of attention during the 1800s and early 1900s, for many circus performers and other daredevils saw them as a challenge. Tightrope walkers, such as the Frenchman Blondin, have walked over the gorge on thin ropes or wires. Sometimes they have carried people and weights as they did so. Some people have gone over the falls in barrels, and a pilot even flew under the nearest bridge. Niagara Falls also is, and has been for years, a popular honeymoon retreat.

Old Faithful

Yellowstone's Old Faithful shoots water into the air about once an hour.

Yellowstone National Park is a land of thousands of geysers. The word *geyser* sounds like *gusher*. And gushing is exactly what happens. First, there is a rumble, a deep noise from under the earth. Then a little water slops over the spout that has built up around the mouth of the geyser. Next there is a roar, as hot water and steam come shooting out of the geyser, sometimes hundreds of feet into the air.

There were volcanoes here long ago that forced hot liquid rock up from deep within the ground. That magma is still here, and it superheats surface water that seeps into the ground. It is that superheated water that shoots forth from Yellowstone's geysers.

Old Faithful is a big geyser, but not the biggest. However, it is by far the best known, because it really is an "old faithful." You can count on it to blow its jet of water and steam into the air every hour or two, which is much more frequent than most geysers, many of which spout irregularly, and as little as once or twice a week. Sometimes, the geyser is "only" about 100 feet high, but it has been known to reach 180 feet. Sometimes, Old Faithful will throw as much as 8,000 to 10,000 gallons of water and steam high into the air in just a few minutes.

Besides Old Faithful, Yellowstone National Park boasts about three hundred other geysers, and thousands of hot springs, steam holes, hot mudholes, and hot lakes. The park is mostly in northern Wyoming, but spills over into Montana and Idaho as well. Yellowstone was one of America's first national parks. It was set up by an act of Congress in 1872. The area was Indian country long before that. American explorers and trappers such as John Colter and Jim Bridger first came here in the early 1800s.

Yellowstone has a great deal more than geysers and other hot places. Here also is the huge Grand Canyon of the Yellowstone. The Yellowstone River has carved great waterfalls far higher than those at Niagara. Much of the park is on a cool, raised plateau, about 7,000 to 8,000 feet above sea level. It is the home of the grizzly bear, black bear, elk, cougar, deer, mountain sheep, coyote, and a dozen other kinds of animals. People visiting Yellowstone are warned not to feed the bears, but many do anyway. Black bears live near the roads entering Yellowstone, so visitors often see bears standing on their hind legs and walking up to the windows of cars, seeking food.

Olympic Rain Forest

In the lush Olympic Rain Forest, everything is covered with green.

The huge Olympic Rain Forest extends along fifty miles of wild seacoast. It is part of the Olympic National Park, which covers over a thousand square miles of the Olympic Range in Washington State.

The Olympic Rain Forest is some of the rainiest country in the United States. For most of the year, a wet wind comes in almost every day off the Pacific, bringing rain and fog. All that wetness, though, also brings mild temperatures. The combination of warmth and wetness helps build rich, deep soil, and makes the beautiful rain forest here grow. Most widespread are the thick, moss-covered hemlock and spruce trees. Many of them are over two hundred feet tall. Large maples and cottonwoods are found here, too. Their broad leaves join together high over the forest, forming a sort of forest ceiling called a canopy. When you visit the forest, you walk on a carpet of soft mosses and ferns of all sizes and shapes. You can find many different kinds of mushrooms, too, growing up from the forest floor. But they are for looking at, not eating, for many are quite poisonous.

The Olympic Rain Forest is a safe haven for many animals and birds. On the coast, you can see seals, sea lions, and sea otters, along with such birds as bald eagles, great blue herons, and gulls. Inland, you can find herds of big Roosevelt elks. They live up in the mountains in warm weather, but when the weather turns cool, they come down to live in the forest. Such animals as deer, beavers, black bears, bobcats, rabbits, raccoons, and squirrels also live in the forest and on the mountain slopes above. And there are many different kinds of birds—mountain bluebirds, rosy finches, hummingbirds, and the thrushes, whose song is so lovely to hear.

Percé Rock

This huge limestone rock stands in the sea, far north in Canada's province of Quebec. It stands at the natural entrance to North America from Europe—the end of the Gaspé Peninsula, in the Gulf of St. Lawrence. On the mainland is the French Canadian fishing village of Percé. The huge rock is connected to the mainland, but you can walk to it only in low tide. At other times the connection is covered with water.

Percé Rock is a very big rock indeed. It is about one-third of a mile long and almost three hundred feet high. It is called Percé because it is cut through, or "pierced," by a large arch. The French word for "pierced" is *percé*.

Percé Rock is home to large flocks of seabirds, especially gannets. And the rock itself offers a fascinating record of natural history. Buried in the rock are the fossil traces of creatures that lived millions of years ago. Because Percé Rock is constantly exposed to the action of the water and its tides, layer after layer of rock erodes away, exposing more and more fossils from the past.

Percé Rock is one of Canada's best-known natural wonders. Every year, people come from all over Canada to drive and vacation on the beautiful Gaspé Peninsula. For them, a view of and perhaps a walk over to Percé Rock is a "must." It is an especially proud place for French Canadians, for the great early French explorers came this way, past Percé Rock, on their way to the St. Lawrence River and on into North America.

At the mouth of the St. Lawrence River, Percé Rock stands guard.

Petrified Forest

Over millions of years, what was once a tree became a rock.

It looks like wood—part of a cut tree trunk. But there are bright colors inside—and no wood ever had colors like these. Well, it was wood once. But over a long period of time it has petrified—that is, turned into stone. Not just any old stone, either. This is stone shot through with amber, amethyst, iron, and other beautifully colored minerals, all mixed up with one another. The resulting petrified wood has all the colors of the rainbow. When the hot, bright sun shines on a field of petrified tree trunks, it is one of the most unusual sights in the world.

You can cut a small piece of petrified wood and buff it to a high, bright polish. The result is a beautiful work of art. It had better be a small piece, by the way. Petrified wood is as heavy as stone, because that is what it is now. A piece that does not look very big may actually weigh hundreds of pounds.

Petrified Forest National Park is in Arizona. Here are the remains of many thousands of petrified tree trunks. Most of them were originally a kind of pine. Perhaps 160 million years ago, they lived on a flat, well-watered plain. Dinosaurs and many other early plants and animals lived there, too. But over a long period of time these trees died. They were then carried off by floods and came to rest many miles away, in this place. Over many millions of years, they were covered with earth and slowly turned to stone, as silica—which this stone is made of—gradually replaced their wood. That happened to many other plants, dinosaur remains, and other animals here, too.

Later, this land rose, and wind and water gradually exposed layer after layer of these petrified tree trunks and the remains of dinosaurs and other plants and animals, all turned to stone.

Pikes Peak

One of the finest and most famous of American sights is the great front range of the Rockies. Coming from the east, across the wide western plains, on a clear day you can see the mountains loom up from fifty, even one hundred miles away. At first, because you are so far away, they do not look very big. But as you get closer, they stop looking like hills. Then they start looking like the huge mountains they really are.

In a fast modern car, that all happens in just a couple of hours. But before there were cars, pioneers and prospectors crossed the plains on foot, in wagons, and on horseback. Then those mountains grew and grew for days, bigger and bigger each day, full of promise and mystery.

Coming across the plains in southern Colorado, what people saw first was huge Pikes Peak, named after Lieutenant Zebulon Pike, who discovered it in 1806. It stood alone, a fourteen-thousand-foot-high mountain a little in front of the rest. What it became—for all the pioneers and prospectors of early times in the West—was a landmark and a goal. When they were traveling hard, far across the plains and a thousand miles from home, their slogan was "Pikes Peak or Bust!" If they could make it to Pikes Peak, they would find water, firewood, shelter from sun and storms, fish in the streams, game to hunt, and maybe gold.

This was the country of the Ute Indians before the pioneers came. In those times, the mountain was a Ute holy place.

Pikes Peak was a welcome sight to pioneers crossing the Great Plains.

Point Reyes

British sailor Sir Francis Drake explored Point Reyes over four hundred years ago.

You cannot quite see China, looking east from high atop these headlands. But that speck of a ship you see far out in the shipping lanes may well be headed for China, many thousands of miles away across the Pacific Ocean. Or perhaps it is going to Hawaii, or Southeast Asia, or north to Alaska. Looking west from Point Reyes, the world is very, very wide.

Point Reyes is thirty-five miles north of San Francisco, on one of the most beautiful stretches of coastline in North America. It is one of those places where the highlands come right down to the sea, with huge numbers of seabirds, and the surf crashing in night and day.

The harbor here is called Drakes Bay. British explorer Sir Francis Drake and his crew put in here in their ship, the *Golden Hind*, in 1579. He thought he was the first European to explore this coast. Actually, Spanish explorers had been here before him. Drake claimed this land for England, but California was to be Spanish, not English. Then, in the 1840s it became part of the United States.

At Point Reyes, you will see all the birds and sea creatures native to the California coast. Many California sea lions live here, and when they "speak," they sound just like dogs barking. Many of the larger northern sea lions and families of sea otters live here, too. The sea otters were once hunted for their furs, and nearly all of them were killed. But in recent years they have been protected against hunters. Many kinds of birds live at Point Reyes, too—gulls, cormorants, pelicans, oystercatchers, sea ducks, and even sometimes a black-footed albatross, with its seven-foot wingspan.

Saguaro National Monument

America's largest cactus is the saguaro, like this one in Arizona.

During their rare bloomings, the saguaros bring beauty to the desert.

Many kinds of cactuses grow in the deserts of the American Southwest. The biggest of them all is the giant saguaro cactus, which often grows fifty feet high. When you are in a place where many saguaros grow together, it is like being on a different planet, in a forest of giant, spiky creatures.

There is such a place, and it is not on a different planet. It is in Arizona. There you can find a big grove of saguaros that is one of the most unusual forests on earth. It has been set aside as the Saguaro National Monument, for it is very much worth saving. And saguaros need saving.

They are very large, and look very tough. But they are really very delicate plants.

All desert plants, and certainly saguaros, are very good at holding water. They could not live very long in the desert without doing that. So lack of water is not the saguaro's problem. Nor is it lack of seeds to grow new saguaros. Each plant scatters millions of seeds. And each of those seeds might grow into a huge saguaro. The great problem, though, is that mice and other desert creatures find saguaro seeds and tiny saguaro plants absolutely delicious. And saguaros take a very long time to grow large. A saguaro seed that takes root may spend fifteen years growing a few inches high. It may need another fifteen years before it grows its strong spiky protective coat. All during those years, it is at risk of being eaten by one of those desert creatures. And even huge, full-grown saguaros can be infected by bacteria that attack them from inside.

Fortunately, many saguaros do survive. When they do, they can live as long as 150 to 200 years. Mountain man Kit Carson and the Indian chief Geronimo may have walked among some saguaros that we can still see today in the Arizona desert.

Sequoia

The huge General Sherman sequoia weighs well over two thousand tons.

America's huge sequoias are some of the world's best-known trees. For example, the General Sherman Tree in California's Sequoia National Park is 270 feet high, weighs about 4.5 million pounds, and is still growing. It is probably the heaviest tree in the world.

The General Sherman Tree is approximately 2,500 years old. Some living sequoia trees are even older—perhaps as much as 3,500 to 4,000 years old. These California sequoias were living at the time the ancient Egyptian pyramids were being built.

What makes the sequoias so amazing is not only their height and the spread of their branches. Some Douglas firs on the West Coast grow even taller. But unlike other trees, the sequoia's thickness is uniform for its full height.

Sequoias do not taper at trunk and branch, but are as big and heavy at the top and branch as they are at ground level. A sequoia branch far up in the tree can be as thick as the trunks of many other trees. And they keep on growing. A tree like the General Sherman Tree grows as much new wood every year as other trees grow to attain full size.

There were once far more sequoias than there are today. Only twenty thousand or so are still alive. Their wood was much prized and their existence was once threatened by logging. But today they are protected in such places as Sequoia National Park. Now they are free to grow as long as the thousands of years they live, as part of our national heritage.

Valley of the Dinosaurs

Dinosaurs once flourished here, living on the shore of an inland sea.

About seventy-five million years ago, this place out in Canada's province of Alberta was on the shore of a warm sea that covered the center of North America. The climate was warm, with a great deal of rain, and heavy tropical vegetation grew along the coast of the sea.

Dinosaurs lived here then—lots of dinosaurs, and of many, many kinds. They lived out their lives, died here, and left their bones in what was then soft mud and sand.

Then, over millions of years, that mud and sand turned into layers of hard shale and sandstone. The dinosaur bones—sometimes whole dinosaur skeletons—were encased in that mud and sand, where they hardened, too, into fossils. Trees, plants, seashells, and many other things that used to be on the shore of that old sea—all of them, too, turned into fossils.

Later, about sixty million years ago, the land dried out and rose. That was part of the same geological change that made the Rocky Mountains rise. Still later, it became the near desert it is today.

Over tens of millions of years, wind and weather have worn away the land here. As that has happened, the old dinosaur bones and other fossils have been exposed—millions of them. In 1884, people began discovering dinosaur bones in the valley—and later whole dinosaur skeletons. By now, hundreds of dinosaur skeletons and many other fossils have been found—so many that the place has come to be called the Valley of the Dinosaurs. Part of this valley is Alberta's Dinosaur Provincial Park, where visitors can see many of the best of the dinosaur and other fossil remains.

47

Virginia Falls

The far north's Virginia Falls is even higher and larger than Niagara.

Virginia Falls, on the Nahanni River, in Canada's Northwest Territories, is one of the most powerful and beautiful waterfalls in North America. The main falls plunges 316 feet, over half again as far as Niagara Falls, and carries a huge amount of water over its crest to crash down on the rocks below. It is part of Nahanni National Park, which covers over 1,800 square miles of unspoiled northern wilderness.

Virginia Falls is only one of many waterfalls along the 375-mile course of the Nahanni River. During the course of its wild ride downhill, the river plunges about three thousand feet, falling over three hundred feet at once at Virginia Falls.

Early in its course, the Nahanni River passes through hot springs that keep the water there at almost one hundred degrees. On its way, the river goes through four huge, deep canyons, one

of which—the Third Canyon—has walls 3,500 feet high. Below Virginia Falls are miles of white-water rapids.

Many kinds of birds, fish, animals, and plants live on the Nahanni. Here you can see over one hundred different kinds of birds, including the rare golden eagle and the trumpeter swan. Trout, arctic grayling, and a dozen other kinds of fish swim in the river. Grizzly bears, black bears, beavers, wolves, caribou, and about three dozen other kinds of animals live free in this wild country.

Here, too, and especially at the hot springs, you can find flowers normally found only far to the south, like asters and lady's slippers. And at the hot springs near Virginia Falls, wild orchids blossom beside the northern snow.

White Sands

Here, in southern New Mexico, are some of the most unusual sand dunes in the world. They are not a gray or light brown, like the sand you find on a beach by the ocean. Nor is their sand made of tiny, hard pieces of rock—bits that you cannot finally break any smaller—like most sand. The sand here is fine, and pure white. If you rub it, it will turn into a fine powder and all but disappear.

There is another difference, too. If you put ordinary sand into a hot enough fire, it will turn into glass. And if you put it into water, it will just get wet and sink to the bottom. But if you put this kind of sand into a fire, it will bake hard. The result is plaster of Paris, which some sculptors use to make figures. And if you put it into water, it will dissolve just as sugar does

The difference between this and other sand is that ordinary sand is made of one kind of material, called silica. This sand is made of another material, called gypsum. These huge dunes in New Mexico's White Sands are made of pure gypsum. The weather has ground it down into the finest, softest, whitest sand to be found anywhere in the world. In the hot sun, gypsum is cooler to the touch than ordinary sand, too.

The gypsum sands were carried here by wind and water from the mountains surrounding this place. And, like all sand dunes, they move. They gradually shift as the wind pushes sand over the top of each dune. It seems as though they are shifting just a little. But beware these gypsum sands. If you park too close to them, and the wind comes up, your car could quickly be up to its hubcaps in soft, heavy sand.

New Mexico's White Sands are made of powdery gypsum, not ordinary sand.

Yosemite

Looming over Yosemite is the great granite block called Half Dome.

If you go out to California's Yosemite National Park in the spring, you will see the highest waterfalls in North America. A huge wall of white water comes pouring down to crash with a tremendous roar at the foot of the falls. Yosemite Falls is 2,435 feet high. It takes a straight drop of 1,430 feet before tumbling down several hundred feet of white-water rapids, and finally dropping straight down again 320 feet. In all, it is thirteen times as high as Niagara.

Like the many other waterfalls in the park, Yosemite Falls is fed by the melting snow of the high Sierra Nevadas—Spanish for "Snow-clad Mountains." Some mountains in the park are over thirteen thousand feet high. And in winter, the snow in the high passes is often over ten feet deep. So in the spring, the park's falls are full of water. Some of them, although not as high as Yosemite, are still among the highest waterfalls in North America. Ribbon Fall, for example, falls straight down over 1,600 feet, and Bridalveil Fall, over six hundred feet. But by late summer, most of the park's falls, including Yosemite Falls, are dry or almost dry.

Yosemite Park has a great deal more to offer than its beautiful waterfalls, though. The whole Sierra Nevada Range is a huge block of granite. It was thrust up out of the ground by forces working deep within the earth. Over millions of years, wind, water, glaciers, and forces working within the earth have all cut and shaped Yosemite, creating a beautiful mountain valley seven miles long and almost a mile wide. It was cut by the Merced River, which was helped by the grinding action of the glaciers that were here long ago.

The biggest single thing in the valley is also the biggest single granite block in the world. That is El Capitán, the over 7,500-foot-tall mountain at one end of the valley. At the other end is a large rounded granite mountain called Half Dome, nearly nine thousand feet high. Some of the other well-known rock formations here are Cathedral Rocks, Inspiration Point, and Glacier Point.

Yosemite supports a great deal of animal and plant life. The huge Grizzly Giant sequoia tree in Mariposa Grove is almost one hundred feet around, over two hundred feet high, and almost four thousand years old. There are many other big sequoias here, too. You can also see such trees as ponderosa pines, incense cedars, and Douglas firs. And in the high fields you can see the mountain flowers—lilies, phlox, columbines, and more.

When this was Indian country, Yosemite was home to many California grizzly bears and mountain lions. The grizzlies are gone now and few mountain lions remain. But you can still see black bears, wolverines, beavers, raccoons, weasels, porcupines, and skunks. Many kinds of birds live here, too—kingfishers, quails, grouses, and purple finches are just a few of them.

Though dry part of the year, Yosemite Falls is the highest in North America.

All of these—the animals, flowers, trees, mountains, waterfalls—are protected. For they are all within the confines of Yosemite National Park. We owe this park and many others to the people who have fought to preserve our natural wonders for us—and for all those who come after us. We owe Yosemite especially to naturalist John Muir. He came here in 1868, and from then on tirelessly fought to preserve this wonderful place. In 1890, he succeeded, and Yosemite became a national park.

Acknowledgments

We are grateful to Domenico Firmani for his always-expert help on this book. As photo researcher, he has reached out around North America and beyond for just the right pictures of these beautiful American places. We also thank the many people and organizations who allowed us to use their photographs. Their names are detailed in the Photo Credits.

We also very much appreciate the help of the people at the Chappaqua Library—Director Mark Hasskarl, the reference librarians, including Mary Platt, Paula Peyraud, Terry Cullen, Martha Alcott, and Carolyn Jones, and the whole circulation staff, among them Caroline Chojnowski, Jane McKean, and Marcia Van Fleet. They and the staff of Westchester's Interlibrary Loan System have been unfailingly helpful.

Thanks finally to our editor at Atheneum, Jonathan Lanman, and to our publisher, Judy Vantrease Wilson, for their support of this introduction to the natural wonders of America.

Photo Credits

INDEX